COLE PORTER

Twentieth Century Composer
of Popular Songs

BY PAUL SALSINI

B. S. Marquette Univ. Col. of Journalism

D. Steve Rahmas, *A. B., J. D., Columbia U., Editor*

Compiled with the assistance of the Research Staff
of SamHar Press.

SamHar Press
Charlotteville, N.Y. 12036
A Division of Story House Corp.

1972

Salsini, Paul
    Cole Porter, 20th Century Composer of Popular Songs.
Charlotteville, N. Y., Story House Corp. (Samhar Press) 1972.

    31p. 22cm. (Outstanding Personalities, no. 41)
Bibliography: p. 30-31

    1. Porter, Cole 1893-1964 2. Composers- American 3. Music-
Biography (Series: Outstanding Personalities)

MT410.P6.S3   927.84

(The above card has been cataloged by the editor and may not be
identical to that of Library of Congress. Library card portrayed above
is 80% of original size.)

Preassigned Library of Congress Catalog Card Number: 72-89206

COLE PORTER

Twentieth Century Composer
of Popular Songs

As the lights slowly dimmed in the New Century Theater, an expectant hush bristled across the smartly dressed first night audience. Settling in their cushioned seats as the overture began, some theatergoers smirked cynically to their companions; the old Broadway types were almost daring the new musical comedy to be a success. Others wrinkled their programs nervously, fearful that the excellent reviews from Philadelphia had oversold New York's expectations and that the audience would leave the theater disappointed. And there were some, too, who could not help but keep their fingers crossed. Wasn't it about time that the dapper, slightly built first-nighter down front had a solid hit?

All Broadway openings, of course, arouse strong emotions, and members of the audience often feel like members of a jury or witnesses to a hanging. The first night, the first judgment, is all-important. But this night--Dec. 30, 1948--was not simply, as the musical's first song proclaimed, "another op'nin' of another show." This was indeed something special.

For that slightly built man was Cole Porter, the supreme sophisticate of American musical comedy, one of the most popular and successful song writers the country had produced. However, he had not had a musical hit in years. Indeed, after a string of successes in the Thirties and early Forties, there was talk up and down Broadway that he could no longer produce a hit. His last show, as the cynics were quick to point out, had run only 75 performances. Despite those rave reviews from Philadelphia, was this going to be another flop?

3

Indeed it was not. For as the curtain rose on designer Lemuel Ayers' evocation of a dusty backstage set, as spotlights turned on Alfred Drake, Patricia Morison and other principals, and as Porter's glorious score filled the theater, even the cynics were soon won over.

Kiss Me, Kate was, as the trade might put it, boffo. In a significant way Cole Porter had laid his career on the line, and he had won.

Certainly the success of *Kiss Me, Kate* was a high point in the life of this musical genius whose career up to its opening had stretched over more than three decades. It had been a life of many high points, but there had also been bitter frustration and agony. Since a tragic accident in 1937 that had crippled both of his legs, Porter had not spent a day without pain.

The accident had not stopped his productivity. Despite the excruciating pain, frequent operations on his legs and long hospital stays, Porter continued to have a new show or film score almost every year. Such popular favorites as "My Heart Belongs to Daddy," "Friendship," "You'd Be So Nice to Come Home To" and "I Love You" joined the hit parade of Porter songs during those years.

And what a list it was! Here was the man who, seemingly effortlessly, turned out such standards as "All Through the Night," "Anything Goes," "Begin the Beguine," "Do I Love You?" "Don't Fence Me In," "Easy to Love," "I Get a Kick Out of You," "I Love Paris," "In the Still of the Night," "It's De-Lovely," "I've Got You Under My Skin," "Just One of Those Things," "Let's Do It," "Love for Sale," "Night and Day," "Rosalie," "True Love," "What Is This Thing Called Love," "You Do Something to Me," "You're the Top."

Kiss Me, Kate alone brought to the public such delights as "Why Can't You Behave?" "Wunderbar," "So in Love," "Were Thine That Special Face," "Too Darn Hot" and "Always True to You in My Fashion."

Sophisticated, urbane, witty: these are the adjectives most often used to describe Cole Porter's songs. Yet his appeal stretched far beyond the bright lights of Broadway and the tinsel world of Hollywood. The year that *Kiss Me, Kate* opened Porter expressed surprise

4

when he learned that five of his earlier songs were already among the country's 35 all-time favorites. It was a record matched only by Irving Berlin.

In those heady days from the Twenties through the Forties when the American musical comedy was being developed as an art form--truely a unique contribution to the world theater--five composers are ranked at the top: Porter, Berlin, George Gershwin, Richard Rodgers, Jerome Kern. And of these five, only Berlin and Porter wrote both the music and the lyrics.

Apart from his distinctive style, Porter stood in contrast to many composers for a more personal reason: Unlike most others, his was not a rags-to-riches story. He was born rich (though not, as he enviously regarded others with more money, "rich-rich"). He produced his first show on Broadway when he was 24, and though it was a flop, he continued to write songs for the amusement of his international set of literary and social figures until he succeeded with a musical hit. A string of other successful shows followed; and even when a particular musical comedy was not a resounding smash there was general agreement that the blame should be placed more on the book--the dialogue, the plot--than on Porter's score. For every musical, Porter usually had one song that was a big popular success.

Such regularity was undoubtedly pleasing to Porter. As orderly about his personal life as he was about his clothes and the beautiful objects and people who surrounded him, Porter had planned on a musical career since childhood; and, of course, he expected it to be a success.

His childhood was spent, however, far from the sophisticated salons of New York and the European cities where he would spend much of his life. Porter was born June 9, 1891, in an unlikely midwestern city, Peru, Indiana, the son of a young druggist, Samuel Fenwick Porter, and his spirited wife, Kate. The influences from the boy's maternal side were considerably stronger than those from his father.

There was the obvious influence of his maternal grandfather, J. O. Cole, for whom the youth was named. The old man was a millionaire, having first made a fortune in the gold mines of California and then some seven million dollars in the soft coal and timber lands of West Virginia. J. O. played his role in the civic affairs of Peru from his 750 acre farm outside the city and kept his hand in the personal life of his daughter, to whom he was closely attached, and that of her only child. J. O. intended his grandson to become a lawyer, and apparently only tolerated the music lessons which Kate insisted that her son should have.

Piano alone took two hours' practice daily, and the boy was also required to travel thirty miles to Marion, Indiana for violin lessons. In contrast to other children of his--or any other--day, young Cole Porter apparently offered little resistance to such regimentation. He even started composing.

At the age of 10, Cole composed something called a "one song operetta," "The Song of the Birds." The following year, inspired by a bird singing outside his window, the boy wrote "The Bobolink Waltz," a piece that so delighted his mother that she went to Chicago and had it published.

Still there was time for fun: swimming at Lake Maxinkuckee, playing pranks (a habit he developed into an art form in later years) and, for particular enjoyment, visits to the theater and the circus; for Peru had become the winter headquarters for one of the big tops.

At home there were strained relationships. Old J. O. Cole had such a dominating personality that Samuel Porter was effectively removed from family decision making. Kate attempted to bridge the gap, but in the process she smothered her son with protection. Cole, confused, and his father, frustrated, were not surprisingly in an estrangement that was to last their lives. Samuel Porter's love of poetry may, however, have had some influence on the highly praised lyrics his son wrote for his music. Cole and his mother developed a close relationship.

In the midst of one of the family quarrels, Kate announced that Cole would fulfill her wish that he have an education in the East. At the age of 13, Cole escaped the unpleasantness at home and boarded a train for Worcester Academy in Massachusetts. He did not return home for three years.

At Worcester, Cole underwent rigorous training in the classics and in the art of becoming a gentleman. A small boy who looked several years younger than his classmates, Cole easily made friends through his musical ability. Certainly his fellow students were impressed by any boy who could bring his own upright piano for his room all the way from Peru, Indiana! As they gathered around, Cole would play songs from musical comedies that had toured the area and also perform his own compositions.

Following his graduation from Worcester, two months in Europe introduced Cole to Paris and parts of Germany and Switzerland. It was a more sophisticated youth who returned in the fall of 1909 to enter Yale.

Although J. O. Cole was still insisting on a legal career for young Porter, it was obvious that the youth, who had inherited his grandfather's stubbornness, was more interested in his music. Seated at the piano that was now in his room at Yale, Porter began turning out songs for fraternity smokers, and his name was immortalized for many alumni as the composer of two football fight songs, "Bingo Eli Yale" and "Yale Bulldog Song," still sung today. He became president of the Yale Glee Club, performing his own songs as a soloist on tours to such applause that reviewers urged him to join the vaudeville circuit.

Soon Porter branched out into composing complete scores for musical comedies given by Yale fraternities or the Yale University Dramatic Association. The first, a fraternity initiation play, was *Cora* in 1911, followed by *And the Villain Still Pursued Her* and *The Pot of Gold* in 1912, and *The Kaleidoscope* in 1913. The songs for *The Kaleidoscope* were well received and the *Yale Daily News* declared that the music was superior to that of most Broadway shows.

The shows were frequently literate and funny, but they were obviously designed for a college audience, and the titles of some of the songs give an indication of the level of sophistication: "She Was a Fair Young Mermaid," "It's Awful Hard When Mother's Not Along," "Ha, Ha, They Must Sail for Siberia," "Oh, What a

Pretty Pair of Lovers.''

Porter not only wrote the songs but took a leading role in getting the shows produced, even appearing in some of them. He became part of a theatrically minded group at Yale that also included Monty (then known as E. Montillion) Woolley, who was later to become a celebrated director and critic; and Archibald MacLeish, who was to become a noted poet and playwright. In the fall of 1913, following his grandfather's desires, Porter moved on to the Harvard Law School, but his heart remained at Yale. The following April he was again the composer for the Yale Dramatic Association's show. *Paranoia* was directed by Woolley and its cast included MacLeish.

It was now evident that Porter did not belong in law school. At the suggestion of the Harvard law dean, and at the risk of losing his inheritance, Porter transferred to the school of music, and in 1915 he could boast that he had two songs in Broadway musicals. This was the era before the musical comedy had grown up, when outrageous plots were tied loosely together by songs that were usually contributed by several composers. In Porter's case, his "Esmeralda" was used in *Hands Up,* which had music mostly by Sigmund Romberg, and thus became Porter's first song to appear on Broadway. Another song, "Two Big Eyes," for which Porter wrote only the music, was interpolated in Jerome Kern's *Miss Information* later that year. Both shows were flops, but that failed to discourage the young Cambridge composer.

Porter now had a full-scale Broadway show not only in mind but ready. With T. Lawrason Riggs, another member of the Yale dramatic group, Porter had composed *See America First*, a parody of the super-patriotic style of George M. Cohan, which found its inspiration in the satire of Gilbert and Sullivan.

See America First described a wealthy United States senator who disliked anything foreign, especially the titled Englishman who has attracted his daughter. As the Englishman, Clifton Webb, who had been in vaudeville and was later to become a screen star, made his legitimate debut; but apparently the show had few other distinctions. The show opened on March 28, 1916, and ran for only 15 performances; the critics failed to see the parody and were not impressed by Porter's songs. However, one song, "I've a Shooting Box in Scotland," was retrieved by the dance team of Fred and Adele Astaire and put into their vaudeville act.

The show ended any hopes Riggs had for a musical career. A deeply religious man, he later entered the Roman Catholic priesthood. Porter (who had, incidentally, little religious upbringing or preference) stayed on in New York. His mode of life became established: practicing. music, writing songs, and giving parties.

In 1917, after the United States had entered World War I, Porter sailed to Europe to participate in the work of a relief organization that was distributing supplies at the front. The following year he joined the French Foreign Legion, though that was not as romantic a move as it might sound to Americans familiar with the Legion only through desert movies. As an American serving in the French Army, Porter was placed under the Foreign Legion.

Porter's duties and his activities during this time have been clouded by mystery and exaggeration. His military role apparently did not prevent him from continuing to partake of Paris' social life, and he became known for the parties he gave in his borrowed apartment. And, though unable to tote his upright piano along, he did manage to carry a zitherlike instrument with him to the front, amusing his fellow soldiers with American and French popular music.

After the war Porter settled in Paris, and though his glittering parties continued, he became a student of more serious music. He enrolled at the Schola Cantorum, a rigorous training ground for harmony, counterpoint and orchestration. The classicism he learned there merged with contemporary influences--including jazz--on Porter's later writing.

Porter was now an integral part of a widening circle of American expatriates who loved life--and parties. At one of these parties he met a lively young socialite who was acclaimed as one of the most beautiful women in the world. Linda Lee Thomas, who was about eight years older than Porter, was a native of Louisville, Kentucky, and had previously been married to millionaire playboy E. R. Thomas, whose activities included being publisher of *The New York Morning Telegraph.* Linda received a large settlement when they were divorced in 1912, and she settled in Paris. There she was famed not only for her beauty and her entertaining but for her great taste--in the serving of wine and in her food, in her elegant but simple clothes, and in her friends. Porter was fascinated.

Although he had continued to receive a handsome allowance from his grandfather despite his refusal to become a lawyer, Porter felt that it was not enough to properly maintain Linda in marriage. He decided to sail back to the United States to ask his grandfather for more money. This proved to be a lucky decision, for aboard ship Porter met a Broadway producer, Raymond Hitchcock, who was looking for songs for the third edition of his *Hitchy-Koo* revues. Upon hearing Porter's work, Hitchcock hired him immediately.

Hitchy-Koo of 1919 opened on Oct. 6 and ran for only 56 performances, but it included Porter's first song hit, "An Old Fashioned Garden." This was a sentimental song, atypical Porter, which gave the chorus girls an opportunity to run around in elaborate flower costumes. The royalties helped to make up for J.O. Cole's refusal to increase Porter's allowance. Katie Porter did her bit to help too, giving her son more money so that he could marry Linda. The marriage took place in Paris on Dec. 18, 1919.

For much of the Roaring Twenties, Porter and his wife were leaders in the brilliant--even hedonistic--social life which had captured the theatrical and literary personalities who fled America for Europe. Living like characters in an F. Scott Fitzgerald novel of the period, the Porters could be counted on to have a dazzling array of stars at any party they gave. International social figures Gerald and Sara Murphy or Sir Charles Mendl might be there. Stage stars Tallulah Bankhead or Fanny Brice might be at one party, opera singer Mary Garden at another. And of course Monty Woolley was on hand to give his outrageous views of life. Cole and the well-known party giver Elsa Maxwell became life-long friends and co-conspirators on numerous practical jokes.

In Paris the Porters' home included not only Linda's famous art collection, but such novelties as zebrahide upholstery and a room with platinum wallpaper. In 1923, when J. O. Cole died and Porter received a handsome share of the estate, the Porters were able to take a palazzo in Venice. Here their famous parties included one for 600 guests (and 50 gondoliers for guard duty) and one in which the ballet impressario Sergei Diaghilev brought his entire ballet company to perform in a setting lit by 200,000 candles.

The Porters might also rent a train or engage a special motorcade to take their guests to an exotic location for a party; with one group of friends they took a trip up the Nile on a rented houseboat. There was also speedboating on the canals of Venice and the Porters were said to have discovered the white sands of Antibes, on the French Riviera, long before others in the international set. It was, in short, the kind of life one would expect for a handsome, wealthy, and spirited young American couple in those days after the Great War.

Naturally, Porter's musical career suffered during this period, though he continued to compose. His audiences, however, were mainly the people who came to his parties. In 1920, he succeeded in placing three songs in a London show, *A Night Out,* and in 1922 had three others in *Mayfair and Montmarte,* also in London. Porter also wrote the score for another *Hitchy-Koo* revue in 1922, but it closed out of town in Philadelphia.

Perhaps discouraged by his lack of success in the musical comedy theater, Porter readily accepted an invitation to do a ballet score for *Les Ballets Suedois* in Paris in 1923. The piece, "Within the Quota," told the story of an immigrant in America and was a satire on instant success. Unlike Porter's songs, this was a symphonic jazz composition with New Orleans' influences, several months before George Gershwin won fame for his jazz composition "Rhapsody in Blue." Porter's work was praised at the time but was believed to be lost after the ballet company disbanded in 1925.

11

Discovered decades later in the manuscripts Porter had left to Yale, the ballet was performed in New York in 1970 and won new praise for its freshness and vigor.

There was another discouraging venture into musical comedy in 1927 when producer John Murray Anderson asked Porter to do the music for an edition of the *Greenwich Village Follies*. The show ran only 127 performances, though one song, "I'm in Love Again," did go on to win popularity. Porter was more encouraged the following year when his songs for a French night club act, *La Revue Des Ambassadeurs*, were well received.

Returning to New York, Porter now tried to make a serious attempt to get back on Broadway with a show that had more semblance to a plot than the revue format, though revues--a series of skits and sketches and songs--were still popular. It was natural that this sophisticate who had illuminated Parisian nightlife would be chosen as the composer of a show called *Paris*. Starring the vivacious Irene Bordoni, the show placed few demands on Porter. It was still predominantly a revue, with Miss Bordoni singing Porter's five songs in her hotel suite, accompanied by an eleven piece orchestra that inexplicably surrounded her. The songs, however, included "Let's Do It" in which the invitation to fall in love was compared to the example set by nightingales, canaries, penguins, sponges, oysters, clams, eels, dragonflies, mosquitoes, moths, champanzees, giraffes and even hippopotami. It was the kind of verse for which Porter would become famous: a variety of humorous (and well-researched) images put together in a sophisticated frame. *Paris* opened on Oct. 8, 1928, and ran 195 performances.

The following spring, Porter had a London success. *Wake Up and Dream* was an elaborate revue that included Porter's American hit "Let's Do It" and a new lovely ballad, "What Is This Thing Called Love?" The show won critical approval and a run of 263 performances in London, and it was transferred to New York late in 1929.

Before its New York opening, however, Porter had another show on Broadway. Continuing in his Parisian mood, Porter wrote *Fifty Million Frenchmen* with Herbert Fields contributing the book. It was the first of seven shows in which Porter and Fields would collaborate, and the director was Porter's old friend from Yale, Monty Woolley. Starring William Gaxton, *Fifty Million Frenchmen* contributed "You Do Something To Me," "You've Got That Thing" and "I Worship You" to the now fast-growing list of Porter's song hits. Turning from sophisticated Paris to the high and low life of New York, Porter next wrote *The New Yorkers*, described as "a sociological musical satire." The cast featured Jimmy Durante, along with his partners Lew Clayton and Eddie Jackson, and the score included "Take Me Back to Manhattan" and "I Happen to Like New York." But the song that achieved the most attention was "Love for Sale" in which Porter so honestly described the feelings of a young woman of the streets that the critics were aghast. Although it was sung in night clubs, the song was banned from radio. Because of this, Porter always had a special affection for the song.

The New Yorkers, which opened Dec. 8, 1930, had a run of only 168 performances, but it set the pattern for the sophisticated musical comedies that would put Porter apart from other composers during the Thirties. In a special way, Porter achieved the peak of his popularity during this decade, a time when the nation was seeking the kind of urbane escapism that he offered. While other composers indicated the desperation of the times with such songs as "Brother, Can You Spare a Dime," Porter's sparkling men and women were wearing evening gowns, top hats and tails and declaring "I Get a Kick Out of You," "Just One of Those Things," "Begin the Beguine," "Ridin' High" and, reflecting Porter's view of life in general during those gloomy times, "Anything Goes."

Fred Astaire, who captured the essence of Porter's sophistication, starred in *Gay Divorce*, the next Broadway show which proclaimed "Songs by Cole Porter." It was Astaire's first show since his sister and co-partner Adele had fled the stage to marry an English lord, and it had a decidedly weak book, about an unhappy wife's attempts to win a divorce. Nevertheless, Astaire and Claire Luce sang one of Porter's most haunting melodies, "Night and Day." This was an unusually long song, with a chorus of 48 instead of the usual 32 bars. For the music, Porter claimed he was inspired by a Mohammedan chant he had heard in Morocco; some of the lyrics were allegedly inspired by Mrs. Vincent Astor's irritation over the "drip, drip, drip" of rain during one of Porter's visits to her home. This kind of beat was repeated in the song, and singers at first resisted such a difficult melody. However, records of "Night and Day" were soon at the top of the best seller lists. With such other popular delights as "How's Your Romance" and "I Still Love the Red, White and Blue," *Gay Divorce* had a run of 248 performances.

Another symbol of sophistication of the Thirties, Gertrude Lawrence, starred in Porter's next musical effort, *Nymph Errant*, the witty adventure of an amoral British schoolgirl. Presented in London by the famous British producer Charles B. Cochran, *Nymph Errant* enchanted worldly Londoners with such songs as "Experiment" and "It's Bad for Me" and the show-stopping "Physician" with its numerous double-entendres. *Nymph Errant* ran for 154 performances after it opened on Oct. 6, 1933.

Returning to New York, Porter had his biggest hit of the Thirties--both critically and with the public--with his next show: *Anything Goes* was, in fact, the biggest hit of the year. It united for the first time Howard Lindsay and Russel Crouse as a play writing team and it brought Cole Porter and Ethel Merman together for the first of the five shows they would do together. Most of all, however, it is remembered for Porter's songs, a score which most critics rank as second only to his *Kiss Me, Kate*.

The producer, Vinton Freedley, who had presented many of George Gershwin's musicals in the Twenties, first thought of the idea for the show. It would deal with outlandish characters aboard a pleasure ship and he had Miss Merman, William Gaxton and Victor Moore in mind for the leads. The team of P. G. Wodehouse and

Guy Bolton was at first engaged to write the libretto; but the story they turned out, involving a shipwreck, turned out to be useless when a real cruise ship, the *S. S. Morro Castle*, burned and went down off Asbury Park, New Jersey, with a loss of 134 lives. Freedley now enlisted Lindsay and Crouse to revise the book. The complicated story they produced, involving gangsters in disguise and shipboard romances, was truly a musical comedy.

Miss Merman, who had stopped Gershwin's 1930 musical *Girl Crazy* when she proclaimed "I Got Rhythm," played the part of Reno Sweeney, a night club singer aboard the ship. Porter was captivated by the trumpet clarity of her voice and responded with the powerful "I Get a Kick Out of You," "You're the Top," "Anything Goes" and "Elow, Gabriel, Blow." Miss Merman stopped the show in the first scene with "I Get a Kick Out of You" and it became a big hit, even though some radio stations objected to the word "cocaine" in the lyrics and insisted that it be changed to "champagne."

"You're the Top" was another of Porter's anthologies in song. Exchanging compliments, Miss Merman and Gaxton compared each other to some 60 superlatives, from Mickey Mouse to an O'Neill drama to Mrs. Astor to Keats to the Tower of Babel. Every line presented a new image--and another laugh. And in the title song Porter declared his own cosmopolitan view of the world going mad: through all of the insanity, Porter remained cool, detached, and sane.

After rave reviews had arrived from the tryout in Boston, *Anything Goes* opened to a dazzled first night audience in New York on Nov. 21, 1934. During its run of 420 performances, Porter became the toast of Broadway. The columnist Walter Winchell crowned him "King Cole Porter" and reporters flocked for interviews. The success that Porter had dreamed of since his days at Yale had arrived.

Soon after the opening of *Anything Goes* Porter teamed up with playwright Moss Hart to write another musical. Perhaps inspired by the nautical theme of *Anything Goes*, they decided to get away from New York and do their writing on a four and a half month cruise that would take them 34,000 miles around the world. As usual, Porter had an entourage that included not only Linda and Hart but also his friends Howard Sturges and Monty Woolley. It was a happy life aboard the *S. S. Franconia* as the group stopped first for parties in Hollywood (where Porter was approached by MGM to write a film score), then on to exotic stopovers in the South Pacific and, upon reaching Africa, a visit to Zanzibar, where Porter arranged an audience with the sultan. Far from being distracted by such diversions, Porter was inspired by what he saw and heard on the cruise. He returned to New York with the score for the new show, *Jubilee,* almost completed. He had, of course, remembered to take an upright piano along.

The plot of *Jubilee* concerned a mythical royal family's adventures after they escape from their thrones and mingle with the common folk. One character was based on Porter's party-giving friend Elsa Maxwell, and the queen herself took up with a Tarzan-like movie star. Mary Boland, Melville Cooper, and June Knight headed the cast, which also included young Montgomery Clift. The score included "Just One of Those Things," which was to achieve long-lasting fame, and "The Kling-Kling Bird on the Divi-Divi Tree," which Porter said was inspired during a stop in Jamaica.

Yet the most enduring song was another haunting Porter melody, "Begin the Beguine," introduced by Miss Knight in her role of the night club singer. Porter said he was inspired by native rhythms he had heard in the Dutch East Indies. "Begin the Beguine," though applauded when *Jubilee* opened on Oct. 12, 1935, did not become a hit until a year later when Artie Shaw recorded it, and soon dancing the beguine became a national rage. Years later Porter declared that "Begin the Beguine" and "Night and Day" were his two best songs.

The show itself did not achieve such lasting fame. Opening night critics, who two evenings earlier had witnessed the history-making opening of Gershwin's *Porgy and Bess,* were not particularly impressed by Porter's score and were already comparing it unfavorably to *Anything Goes.* When Miss Boland left the cast to return to Hollywood, the show folded after a run of

169 performances. Porter, who had invested his own money in the show, never again backed a Broadway musical.

Late in 1935 Porter and his wife abandoned New York for a stay in Hollywood so that he could fulfill his contract for an MGM musical, *Born to Dance*. Porter immediately became immersed in the social life of the film colony but his wife, who suffered from a respiratory ailment, found the climate bad for her health and her husband's new associates dull and often boorish. Porter himself apparently was fascinated by the way a movie was put together and by the powerful influences a producer had on the film process. The score he turned out under unusually trying conditions included two more haunting melodies, "I've Got You Under My Skin" and "Easy to Love," which Porter had originally written for *Anything Goes*. The film, starring Eleanor Powell and featuring James Stewart, was released in 1936.

There was a reunion of sorts for Porter's next Broadway show. Vincent Freedley was again the producer and Howard Lindsay and Russel Crouse wrote the book. Fresh from her triumph in *Anything Goes*, Ethel Merman was starred with Jimmy Durante, who had been in Porter's *The New Yorkers*., The cast also included another comic, Bob Hope.

The show was called *Red, Hot and Blue* and was the kind of brassy entertainment an audience would expect from a Merman-Durante musical. The plot did little to advance musical theater, having to do with the search for a missing heiress with a waffle iron mark on her posterior. The audience didn't seem to mind as long as Miss Merman was singing and Durante was clowning around. The fact that two such superstars were sharing the stage resulted in strained--and well publicized--relations between their agents over how they should be billed in advertisements. Normally, the person listed first, in the left-hand corner, is conceded to be the leading star. The agents finally agreed to an ad that had the names crisscrossed.

Porter's score gave Miss Merman such showcase songs as "Ridin' High," "You're a Bad Influence on Me," the title song, and the jaunty "It's De-Lovely."

17

Apart from such exuberant songs, however, Miss Merman stopped the show nightly sitting under a single spotlight and singing the soulful "Down in the Depths (on the 90th Floor)."

Red, Hot and Blue, which opened Oct. 29, 1936, had a run of only 183 performances, but by the time it closed Porter was back in Hollywood writing another film score for MGM. *Rosalie* starred Nelson Eddy and Eleanor Powell and its title song became an enormous hit. The song was Porter's seventh attempt, all six previous versions having been turned down by the producer in a typical example of Porter's troubles with the film industry. There was another popular song for Eddy in the score, too, "In the Still of the Night."

It appeared, as the Thirties started to draw to a close, that Porter's life had developed a new routine: a Broadway play, then a Hollywood musical, then back to Broadway. Linda was not happy with this arrangement, preferring that he spend all his time on Broadway rather than working in films, and there were periods when their marriage was strained. In the fall of 1937 Porter left the vacationing Linda in Paris when he returned to America to work on a new musical, *You Never Know.*

A few weeks after his arrival, Porter was spending the weekend with friends on Long Island when he decided to go riding. He had not ridden in some time and the horse he chose was a spirited one. As Porter rode over a hill the horse became frightened. Horse and rider went down, with the horse falling on one of Porter's legs. Porter was still caught in the stirrup and as the horse attempted to rise it fell again, this time on the composer's other leg. Finally Porter was freed, but both legs were crushed and he lay stunned but conscious. Friends rushed for help and in those minutes after the accident Porter set an example for himself on how to behave under pain for the rest of his life. He said later that as he lay there he worked on the lyrics for the song "At Long Last Love" for *You Never Know.*

At the hospital Porter was unconscious and doctors determined that both legs were so badly mangled that they should be amputated. Linda, contacted in Paris, knew that her husband would lose the will to live if he lost his legs. She contacted Porter's mother, who agreed, and returned immediately to her husband's side.

At Linda's insistence, amputation was put off and doctors attempted other operations to correct the damage. Porter stayed in hospitals for months as one after another operation was performed. Over the next twenty years he endured some thirty-five operations on both of his legs until he finally submitted to an amputation of one of them in 1958.

Porter was 46 years old when the accident happened. He could boast of a successful career, enormous wealth, a sparkling collection of friends, and a beautiful wife. The accident could have cut him off from all of this; he could have sunk into such deep depression that his life could have been effectively over as of that October morning in 1937.

There were indeed terrifying times in the next decades, periods when the pain was almost impossible to bear. But those who expected Porter to yield to the pain forgot that this was the grandson of stubborn old J. O. Cole and the son of spirited Katie, that this was the soldier who had taken a musical instrument to the front during World War I, the host who seemed to enjoy his own parties more than anyone else, the composer who had turned out such marvelous songs that he reigned as the king of Broadway. Life and his career could not be so easily dismissed.

So Porter pressed on, between his hospital stays, with writing the score for *You Never Know.* It was a depressing venture, with a weak libretto with which to work and backstage wrangling to solve. Tryouts began in March and the show did not open on Broadway until Sept. 21, 1938, with a cast that included Clifton Webb, Libby Holman, and the "Mexican spitfire," Lupe Velez. The critics tore into the show and were not impressed with Porter's songs, which included "At Long Last Love," "You Never Know," "From Alpha to Omega" and "For No Rhyme or Reason." The show closed after 78 performances.

In the cynical, often cruel world of Broadway theater, there were those who said after the opening of *You*

Never Know that Porter's genius was indeed snuffed out by his accident and that he would never again have another hit. They were proven wrong less than two months after that opening, however, when another Porter show opened.

Porter had been working on *Leave It to Me* simultaneously with *You Never Know* and it opened on Nov. 9, 1938. With Vinton Freedley again the producer, *Leave It to Me* had a witty book by Samuel and Bella Spewack and featured Victor Moore as an American ambassador bungling his job in Russia. There were all sorts of topical references and the first act finale had Stalin singing the Communist "Internationale." In those days, with war breaking out in Europe and threatening to engulf the United States, audiences particularly chuckled at the swipes at Nazi Germany.

If not an outright bow, the show was at least a nod to the new social consciousness then having an impact on America's musical theater. An important example had been set in 1937 with Marc Blitzstein's *The Cradle Will Rock,* dealing with the labor movement, a theme also used by Harold Rome in *Pins and Needles.* Rodgers and Hart had ribbed the Roosevelt administration in *I'd Rather Be Right* and the issue of totalitarianism was the theme of Kurt Weill's *Knickerbocker Holiday.*

Besides Moore, the cast also included such stars as Sophie Tucker and William Gaxton, and listed way down in the cast credits was a young dancer, Gene Kelly. However, once the show opened audiences turned their attention to a slender 24 year old girl from Texas who was making her Broadway debut. Just as Ethel Merman became a star by belting out "I Got Rhythm" in *Girl Crazy,* Mary Martin stole *Leave It to Me* every night when she perched on a wardrobe trunk and, in the unlikely setting of a Siberian railroad station, coyly did a striptease while singing "My Heart Belongs to Daddy." There were other popular hit songs, too, including "Get Out of Town," "Most Gentlemen Don't Like Love" and "From Now On." The critics and the public loved the show, ensuring a run of 291 performances.

After the depressing venture into *You Never Know,*

Leave It to Me had a therapeutic effect on Cole Porter, and there was an even bigger hit the following year. *DuBarry Was a Lady* reunited Porter with Ethel Merman, and it also starred the popular comic Bert Lahr. There was no social significance in *DuBarry Was a Lady*; it was big and bawdy and brassy and splashy. Lahr played a night club washroom attendant who dreamed he was Louis XV of France. Miss Merman, playing a night club singer, turned up as the paramour DuBarry in his dreams, and so there were plenty of opportunities for fancy costumes and sets. Miss Merman belted out "Katie Went to Haiti" and "Give Him the Oo-La-La" which contained references to both the French court and Franklin and Eleanor Roosevelt. She joined Lahr to sing a hymn of low life constancy, "Friendship," and there were, of course, a couple of songs filled with double entendres, "But in the Morning, No" and "It Ain't Etiquette." In one sequence a young dancer, Betty Grable, sang another popular song, "Well, Did You Evah?" The show opened on Dec. 6, 1939, and ran for 408 performances.

As the final musical to open on Broadway during the Thirties, *DuBarry* was the kind of show, filled with laughs and songs and dances, that provided an escape for a nation on the verge of a world war. In the Forties, as the country plunged into the war, Porter's brand of musical comedy continued to be popular, both on Broadway and in films.

Sufficiently recovered from his accident, Porter again made annual treks to California where the warm sun, leisure living and pleasant companions helped in his recovery. During one stay, he turned out five songs for another MGM musical, *Broadway Melody of 1940*. It starred Fred Astaire and Eleanor Powell and the big highlight was a production number to "Begin the Beguine."

Audiences were mindful of the war in Europe when Porter opened his next Broadway show, *Panama Hattie*, on Oct. 8, 1940. The spy plot dealt with attempts to blow up the Panama Canal, but there was nothing serious about the way it was handled. Ethel Merman was again the star and again cast in her now familiar role of a night club singer. Outfitted in outlandish attire, she took command of the stage with such songs as "I've Still Got My Health," "Make It Another Old-Fashioned, Please" and "Fresh as a Daisy." However, the surprise hit of the show was a sentimental number that was definitely un-Porterish. Audiences choked up when Miss Merman joined eight year old Joan Carroll for a duet, "Let's Be Buddies"; *Panama Hattie* chalked up 501 performances.

Porter was now plunged back into his old work schedule. Despite constant pain and the need for more hospital stays and even surgery, he had resumed the kind of life he lived before the accident, at least as far as his work was concerned. His social life was still limited, though a succession of friends came to visit in his New York apartment, in his rented home in California and in the large house Linda had found in Massachusetts.

Porter went back to California for another Fred Astaire movie, *You'll Never Get Rich*. It was released in 1941 and its score included "Since I Kissed My Baby Goodbye," "Dream Dancing" and "So Near and Yet So Far."

Back on Broadway, Porter's next show reflected the war interest with its story of three married women and their involvement with three young servicemen. *Let's Face It!* is remembered now as being the first starring vehicle for Danny Kaye, but the cast also included Eve Arden, Vivian Vance, and Nanette Fabray. Although the songs, which included "Farming," "Ace in the Hole" and "You Irritate Me So," were not as memorable as earlier Porter efforts, the show became the third longest running of his career, compiling 547 performances after it opened on Oct. 29, 1941.

The adventurous producer Michael Todd teamed up with Porter for his next show. On the theory that a record of four hits with Ethel Merman could be improved with another attempt, Miss Merman was again the star. *Something for the Boys* gave even Miss Merman a formidable challenge: it cast her as a *former* night club singer, now defense worker, who receives radio messages through the fillings of her teeth. There were several bouncy numbers, including "The Leader of a Big Time Band" and "He's a Right Guy," but the show stopper had Miss Merman and Paula Lawrence in Indian costumes and singing "By the Mississinewah," the tale of a *menage a trois*-- in a tent, no less-- by the "Miss-iss-iss-iss-iss-iss-inewah." The show could boast a run of 422 performances after it opened on Jan. 7, 1943.

A year later, on Jan. 28, 1944, Porter opened a show with a south of the border theme. Produced by Todd, *Mexican Hayride* had comic Bobby Clark, famed for his painted-on eyeglasses, involved with June Havoc, cast as a lady bullfighter. The songs reflected the Mexican mood, including "Sing to Me, Guitar" and "Carlotta" but the one that lingered longest for audiences was a song they could hardly have expected from Cole Porter. Old friend Monty Woolley had dared him to write a song with the simple sentiment "I Love You" and Porter's answer to the challenge became an enormous hit.

Neither *Something for the Boys* nor *Mexican Hayride* appeared to be major efforts for Cole Porter and the belief was growing that Porter--who was 50 years old in 1941--could no longer achieve the eminence he had enjoyed in the Thirties.

Certainly his next two shows did nothing to dispel that belief. In 1944 he wrote songs for a revue, *Seven Lively Arts*. Though it had sketches by George S. Kaufman and Moss Hart, and though its cast included Beatrice Lillie and Bert Lahr, the show lasted only 183 performances. In 1946 Porter wrote the score for Orson Welles' *Around the World in Eighty Days*. Based on the Jules Verne adventure novel, the super production lasted only 75 performances. In 1948 Porter's score for an MGM musical, *The Pirate*, impressed few people and neither did the film, which starred Judy Garland and Gene Kelly.

Porter's own story was now also on view on movie screens. Recognizing the dramatic events of his life, Hollywood chose to film a biography filled with his songs. The result, appropriately called *Night and Day*, was, in the tradition of Hollywood biographies, a much romanticized version. Although Porter and his friends did not admire the movie, which had Cary Grant as Cole and Alexis Smith as Linda, the movie served to re-introduce a dozen Porter standards to the American public.

It was perhaps significant that Porter did not write a single new song for *Night and Day*. In the mid-1940s there were not many reasons for inspiration. He had always worked best when assigned to do a show or a movie, and now there were no assignments. Producers, it was rumored, did not want to take a chance on Porter.

Porter had to face the fact that the American musical theater had been drastically changed during the Forties. It had been a gradual development, to be sure, with *Show Boat*, *Of Thee I Sing* and *Porgy and Bess* outstanding landmarks as the musical progressed from operetta through musical comedy to musical play. In 1943 the historic opening of Rodgers and Hammerstein's *Oklahoma!* declared that the musical could never again really go back to the old form. Songs were now to be truly integrated into the story, advancing the plot. While there would always be comic moments, there was a new approach that would allow composers to deal with serious themes, even, as in *Carousel* and *West Side Story*, tragedy and death.

Porter had never been called upon to write this kind of a show. His had been purely escapist entertainment, frankly designed for the tired businessman. There were strands of a plot but more than that there were jokes and laughs and comic sequences. There were big name stars--Astaire, Merman, Durante, Lahr--who attracted huge crowds. And most of all there were Porter's songs which were allowed to stop, even interrupt, the show. It was no accident that people remembered the songs long after the names of the shows were forgotten.

Porter was understandably reluctant when Sam and Bella Spewack, who had written the book for *Leave It to Me*, approached him to write the music for a new show they were thinking about. After all, the Spewacks were planning a musical *play*, not a musical comedy. And the basis was going to be *Taming of the Shrew*, though Shakespeare could expect only a perilous reception at the box office. Moreover, the producers, Saint Subber and Lemuel Ayres were inexperienced and, when the show was finally on the boards after financial support was painfully obtained, there were no big name stars in the cast.

Despite all these handicaps, *Kiss Me, Kate* turned out to be, in the words of many critics, a perfect musical. The Spewacks, using the play-within-a-play device, had an acting company trying out the *Shrew* in Baltimore. The principals of the acting company were a divorced, but still in love, couple and the action neatly shifted back and forth from Shakespeare's medieval Padua to the Spewacks' modern Baltimore.

Once captivated by his colleagues' enthusiasm and determination, Porter produced one glorious song after another, so many in fact that the Spewacks finally had to tell him to stop. The seventeen numbers finally used were of many moods and rhythms, songs that developed the plot and added dimensions to the characters. In the Shakespearean sections, Petruchio described his search for a wife in "I've Come to Wive it Wealthily in Padua," remembered his past in "Where Is the Life That Late I Led?" and agreed to marry Katherine even though she was not what he expected in "Were Thine That Special Face." The headstrong Katharine expressed her view of life in "I Hate Men" but, in finally yielding to Petruchio, sang a song in which Porter used Shakespeare's own lines, "I Am Ashamed That Women Are So Simple." Meanwhile, in steamy Baltimore, the producer-actor Fred Graham and his ex-wife Lilli, remembered a former show in "Wunderbar" and confessed their own love for each other in "So in Love." Other principals carried the mood along with more comic numbers, including "Always True to You in My Fashion," "Too Darn Hot" and "Brush Up Your Shakespeare."

Alfred Drake played the double role of Fred Graham and Petruchio, Patricia Morison was Lilli-Katharine, and Lisa Kirk and Harold Lang were the focus of the subplot. The settings and costumes by Lemuel Ayers, the choreography by Hanya Holm, and the entire production won the cheers of the audience that opening night in December, 1948, and for 1,077 performances after. *Kiss Me, Kate* became one of the longest running musicals in American history. It won the coveted Antoinette Perry award; a touring company ran for three years and the show was translated into eighteen languages. In 1952, it became a movie hit with Howard Keel, Kathryn Grayson, and Ann Miller.

Kiss Me, Kate was Porter's supreme achievement. He had proved that he could write for the musical theater, not just musical comedy. Indeed, *Kiss Me, Kate* is sometimes defined as a light opera. Again, as after the opening of *Anything Goes,* Porter was the toast of Broadway. And this time there was even greater respect for his genius, a respect that deepened as the songs from *Kiss Me, Kate* became enduring hits.

After such a smash, Porter and the public were disappointed by his next show, *Out of This World,* based on the Amphitryon legend of a god in disguise. Again mixing two vastly different periods, Porter provided songs for both a modern American couple and battling Greek gods and goddesses. There were several lovely ballads, including "Use Your Imagination," "Where, Oh Where?" and "I Am Loved." There were also several whose lyrics indicated that the composer who wrote "Let's Do It" in 1928 had not lost his touch. Some critics found in the long list of comparisons in "Cherry Pies Ought to Be You" a similarity to the images of "You're the Top."

After suffering from numerous tryout problems in its writing and production, *Out of This World* opened in New York on Dec. 21, 1950, with the long-legged Charlotte Greenwood making a return to Broadway after a film career. The critics, perhaps expecting another *Kiss Me, Kate,* turned thumbs down and the show closed after 157 performances.

This was a time of depression, and not only because of the failure of the show. Porter's mother, who had watched his career closely and attended his opening nights, died in 1951. Linda, long plagued by a respiratory ailment, was now at times nearly incapacitated by her illness. She grew frail and was at the point of death several times, only to rally. Porter suffered new pains in his legs, resulting in more surgery and more hospital treatments. There were times when he grew despondent. The Cole Porter who was once the life of every party now declined to see his friends.

Nevertheless, he agreed to take on another show, and on March 23, 1953, *Can-Can* opened. Porter was again working in a Parisian locale, giving him an opportunity to write such songs as "I Love Paris," "C'est Magnifique" and "Allez-Vous-En." The show, having to do with can-can dancers, often looked like it had stepped out of a Toulouse-Lautrec poster, and there was considerable praise for its dancers, notably Gwen Verdon. The critics were not entirely impressed, and again compared Porter's songs unfavorably with those for *Kiss Me, Kate,* but the public liked it and word of mouth helped boost its run to a hefty 892 performances. Later *Can-Can* was made into a popular movie starring Frank Sinatra and Shirley MacLaine.

In May, 1954, after being bedridden for a long period, Linda died. Porter, stoically bearing the loss, looked for work and found it in a show based on an old Greta Garbo movie, *Ninotchka*. Modernized, it became *Silk Stockings*, the story of a Russian woman agent who became captivated by capitalism. The setting was again Paris, and Don Ameche, Hildegarde Neff, and Gretchen Wyler were given such songs as "All of You," "Paris Loves Lovers" and the brassy "Stereophonic Sound." Opening on Feb. 24, 1955, *Silk Stockings* had a respectable run of 478 performances. It was later turned into a movie starring Porter's old friend Fred Astaire and Cyd Charisse.

Silk Stockings was the twenty-fourth--and last--Broadway musical Porter was to do. There were, however, two more movies. *High Society* in 1956 was a frolic for Frank Sinatra, Bing Crosby, and Grace Kelly, and it had a big song hit, "True Love." The following year another movie, *Les Girls*, starred Gene Kelly, but there were no hit songs, and Porter's final effort was a dismal television production, *Aladdin,* shown in 1958.

The final years of Porter's life were bitter and sad. He finally had his right leg amputated in 1958 to relieve

27

the pains of chronic osteomylitis and then began the slow process of learning to walk again with an artificial leg and two canes. It was a technique he never really mastered. After lessons four times a week at a rehabilitation hospital he would return exhausted to his plush apartment in New York's Waldorf-Astoria Hotel. His piano remained closed. There were various offers from producers but Porter did not seem interested. He did not even care about what was going on in the theater, which had been his life for decades. He continued to travel from New York to California according to his old routine, but saw few people other than his valet and his secretary. The old friends he did see believed that he waited only to die, indeed was anxious for death to come.

Two days after an operation for the removal of a kidney stone, Cole Porter died in a California hospital on Oct. 15, 1964, at the age of 73. He was buried in Peru, Indiana, with Katie's grave on one side and Linda's on the other.

There were no immediate survivors--except, of course, Cole Porter's marvelous songs. The sheer number of them is staggering. When his lawyers and associates went through his closets after his death, it was determined that he had written close to one thousand songs during his lifetime. Some three hundred were written during his university days alone. Of the remainder, many were destined for shows but never used, for Porter always wrote more songs than were needed. Most often, they were not withdrawn because of a lack of quality but because Porter felt they were not right for the singer or the show. Sometimes, these songs made their way into another show--the lovely "From This Moment On" was taken out of *Out of This World* during its tryout but became a hit when it was used in the film version of *Kiss Me, Kate*. Other songs, however, remained on the shelf.

Considering his output, the fantastic quality of his work is even more impressive. Porter placed an indelible stamp on each of his songs, though each was different from the others. His music showed a great variety: ballads and waltzes, jaunty tunes and classic rhythms, and of course the beguine. He was not afraid to experiment, as in "Night and Day," and each of his melodies is noted for its originality.

In his lyrics Porter expressed the kind of cultured maturity that gave his musical comedies a sophisticated flavor even if their plots contained mere banalities. Like his music, his lyrics were always original, whether expressing simple sentiments as in "I Love You" or "So in Love" or describing a devilish point of view as in "Give Him the Oo-La-La" or "Always True to You in My Fashion." If Porter's shows--until *Kiss Me, Kate*--did not help to advance the musical comedy, Porter's songs gave Broadway a new kind of sophistication.

It was no wonder that Porter's fame grew after his death, with increasing attention given to his standards and his rediscovered songs. An off-Broadway show, *The Decline and Fall of the Entire World as Seen Through the Eyes of Cole Porter,* ran for 13 months after it opened in 1965, and later there were new records, new biographies and new studies of his manuscripts.

Years after his death, it is obvious that Cole Porter's songs will never die. This giant of Broadway has left a legacy that still causes his many fans to declare: "You're the Top!"

SamHar Press

Division of Story House Corp.

BIBLIOGRAPHY

Astaire, Fred. *Steps in Time.* Harper & Brothers, 1959.

Atkinson, Brooks. *Broadway.* The Macmillan Company, 1970.

Eells, George. *The Life That Late He Led.* G. P. Putnam's Sons. 1967.

Engel, Lehman. *The American Musical Theater: A Consideration.* The Macmillan Company, 1967.

Ewen, David. *The Cole Porter Story.* Holt, Rinehart and Winston, Inc., 1965.

Ewen, David. *New Complete Book of the American Musical Theater.* Rinehart and Winston, 1970.

Ewen, David. *Composers for the American Musical Theater.* Dodd, Mead and Company, 1968.

Ewen, David. *George Gershwin: His Journey to Greatness.* Prentice-Hall, Inc., 1970.

Ewen, David. *The Life and Death of Tin Pan Alley.* Funk and Wagnalls Company, Inc., 1964.

Ewen, David. *Panorama of American Popular Music.* Prentice-Hall, Inc., 1957.

Green, Abel, and Laurie, Jr., Joe. *Show Biz: From Vaude to Video.* Henry Holt and Company, 1951.

Green, Stanley. *Ring Bells! Sing Songs!* Arlington House, 1971.

Green, Stanley. *The World of Musical Comedy,* A. S. Barnes and Company, 1968.

Goldberg, Isaac. *Tin Pan Alley: A Chronicle of American Popular Music.* F. Ungar, 1961.

Howard, John Tasker. *Our American Music: A Comprehensive History from 1620 to the Present.* Thomas Y. Crowell Company, 1965.

Hubler, Richard G. *The Cole Porter Story.* World Publishing Co., 1965.

Kimball, Robert, editor. *Cole.* Holt, Rinehart, & Winston, 1971.

Merman, Ethel, as told to Pete Martin. *Who Could Ask for Anything More.* Doubleday & Co., 1955.

Newman, Shirley P. *Mary Martin on Stage.* Westminster Press, 1969.

Rigdon, Walter, editor. *The Biographical Encyclopaedia and Who's Who of the American Theater.* James H. Heineman, Inc., 1966.

Smith, Cecil. *Musical Comedy in America.* Theatre Arts, 1950.

Spaeth, Sigmund. *A History of Popular Music in America.* Random House, 1948.

Taubman, Howard. *The Making of the American Theatre.* Coward McCann, Inc., 1965.